A Kid's Guide to Drawing
the Countries of the World™

How to Draw
France's
Sights and Symbols

Betsy Dru Tecco

The Rosen Publishing Group's
PowerKids Press™
New York

To Sianna, who gives me great joy

Published in 2004 by The Rosen Publishing Group, Inc.
29 East 21st Street, New York, NY 10010

Editor: Frances E. Ruffin
Book Design: Kim Sonsky
Layout Design: Maria E. Melendez

Illustration Credits: Cover and inside by Mike Donnellan.
Photo Credits: Cover and title page (hand) by Arlan Dean; cover and p. 22 (grapes) © Stock Photos/CORBIS; pp. 5, 42 © Owen Franken/CORBIS; p. 9 © Michael S. Yamashita/CORBIS; p. 10 © Nik Wheeler/CORBIS; p. 12 © Bettmann/CORBIS; p. 13 © Erich Lessing/Art Resource, NY; pp. 18, 28 © Archivo Iconografico, S.A./CORBIS; p. 20 © Gail Mooney/CORBIS; p. 24 © Explorer, Paris/SuperStock; p. 26 © Adam Woolfitt/CORBIS; pp. 30, 40 © Index Stock Imagery, Inc.; p. 32 © Hubert Stadler/CORBIS; p. 34 © Dave Bartruff/CORBIS; p. 36 © Philippa Lewis; Edifice/CORBIS; p. 38 © Desjobert Edition Image Bank.

Tecco, Betsy Dru.
How to draw France's sights and symbols / Betsy Dru Tecco.
   p. cm.— (A kid's guide to drawing the countries of the world)
Summary: Presents step-by-step directions for drawing the national flag, grapes, the Eiffel tower, and other sights and symbols of France.
Includes bibliographical references and index.
  ISBN 0-8239-6683-6 (lib. bdg.)
1. France—In art—Juvenile literature. 2. Drawing—Technique—Juvenile literature. 3. France—Juvenile literature. [1. France—In art. 2. Drawing—Technique.] I. Title. II. Series.
  NC825.F73 T73 2004
  743'.83644—dc21

                                                                              2002013510

Manufactured in the United States of America

Contents

Let's Draw France

France has played a great role in changing the course of history. For many centuries, kings and emperors ruled France. Some believe that King Louis XIV was the greatest of them all. He became king as a child in 1643 and ruled for 72 years. His was the longest reign in European history. During his reign, France became the most powerful nation in Europe. However, the French grew tired of endless wars brought about by their kings. The wish to control the world's biggest empire cost France many lives and too much money.

The French began a revolution against the king and all French royalty in 1789. When the revolution ended in 1799, France had become a republic. French citizens had earned the right to elect their government leaders. In 1799, military hero General Napoléon Bonaparte set up a new form of government called the consulate. This government controlled the lives of French citizens, and it gave Napoléon more power than King Louis XIV had had.

Paris has been called the City of Lights. This photograph of the Champs Elysées, Paris's most famous street, was taken during the Christmas holidays.

When Napoléon made himself emperor in 1804, he tried to control all of Europe. He was forced to give up his throne eleven years later, in 1815, when he was defeated at the Battle of Waterloo.

The Third Republic was formed, and it lasted until World War II. When General Charles de Gaulle, a hero of that war, became president of France in 1958, he formed the Fifth Republic, which exists today. The French president chooses a prime minister, who oversees the government. The French parliament is similar to the U.S. Congress.

Throughout history, France has changed the world in many ways. French scientist Louis Pasteur changed and improved world health by teaching people how to avoid catching diseases.

The ideas of French writers such as Voltaire, René Descartes, and Jean-Paul Sartre changed the way people thought about life. It is believed that science fiction writing was begun in France by French author Jules Verne, whose books include *Twenty Thousand Leagues Under the Sea*.

French artists, such as Claude Monet, Pierre-Auguste

Renoir, and Paul Cézanne, changed the art world and the way that people viewed art, with a new style of painting, called impressionism.

If you like art, you will love France and the works by French artists. In this book, you will learn how to draw some of France's most famous landmarks, and its cultural and historical symbols. They will be works of art that you can enjoy. You will need the following supplies to draw the sights and symbols of France:

- A sketch pad
- An eraser
- A number 2 pencil
- A pencil sharpener

These are some of the shapes and drawing terms you need to know to draw the sights and symbols of France:

— Horizontal line

〰 Squiggle

⬭ Oval

▱ Trapezoid

▭ Rectangle

△ Triangle

▰ Shading

| Vertical line

〜 Wavy line

More About France

An important key to France's success is the ground on which French people walk. Much of the country's soil is fertile, which means it is ideal for growing crops and raising livestock. In fact France's agriculture ranks first in western Europe. Some of France's major products are wheat, beef, pork, poultry, wine from grape vineyards, and dairy foods such as milk and cheese. More than 400 different kinds of cheese are made in France.

The land also has plenty of natural resources, such as valuable metals found in rocks, called ores. They include iron ore, aluminum ore, and bauxite ore, which are used to make aluminum and steel for automobiles and airplanes, of which France makes more than any other country. Coal and timber are in good supply, too. In fact France produces many goods, such as high-fashion clothing, perfume, and fine wine. France has the world's fourth-largest economy because so many other countries want to trade for, or buy, these products.

People like to travel to France. The country's mild

These gardens are known as the Ornamental Gardens because of their beautiful designs. They are at Versailles Palace, once the home of King Louis XIV.

climate offers the best of all four seasons, including snowy winters in the mountains and sunny, dry summers along the Mediterranean coast. France has occasional strong winds, called mistrals. Otherwise it is mostly spared from dangerous forms of weather.

The country's famous cities are exciting to visit. Paris is the largest and most popular because it is the center of France's business and culture. Marseille, Lyon, and Lille are next in size but are much smaller than Paris. Each city has its own appeal, just as do the people of France. The French population is more than 60 million people. France is also home to many people who have moved there from other European countries, North Africa, and Arab nations.

French people share many qualities, too. They are proud of their country and its achievements. The French are famous for having what they call *joie de vivre*, or "joy of life." They seek life's pleasures, whether they are found in art, literature, fine foods, fashion, or a favorite hobby. As the French say, *Vive la France*, or "Long live France!"

These sailboats are moored in the Old Harbor in Marseille, a city in southern France with the country's second-largest population.

The Artist Claude Monet

In the Seine River valley is a village named Giverny. A famous French artist named Claude Monet came to live there in 1883, at the age of 43. The peaceful streams, green meadows, and sloping hills of Giverny must have appealed to Monet, who wanted to paint the outdoors.

Claude Monet died in 1926 at age 86, but people still enjoy his work.

Monet was especially interested in the way that sunlight affected the look of natural surroundings, depending on the time of day. He captured these changes by painting the same scene at different times. Many of his masterpieces are of sunny landscapes, such as fields of haystacks and poppies, and water reflecting light. All of his work is bright and colorful.

Monet used a style of painting known as impressionism, which was created in the late nineteenth century. Instead of making exact lines, impressionists such as Monet and fellow Frenchman Pierre-Auguste Renoir freely used their brushes to make small strokes and dabs of oil paint to create a picture. They usually worked outdoors, using small canvases. Monet would even drift down a river on his boat to find new views to paint.

Impressionism got its name from Monet's 1872 painting titled *Impression: Sunrise*. The painting showed a fishing boat in dark, early-morning waters, with a rising orange sun. It was scorned at first. Impressionism became an art form that is still popular with art lovers around the world. People still collect impressionist works. Claude Monet's house still stands at Giverny, as do the beautiful, Japanese-style gardens that he planted there.

Claude Monet created this oil painting, titled *Red Poppies at Argenteuil*, in 1873, during a visit to the French town of Argenteuil.

Map of France

Map of the Continent of Europe

France is the largest country in western Europe. It is almost the size of Texas. To the west are the Atlantic Ocean and the Bay of Biscay. The English Channel is to the north. The Mediterranean Sea lies southeast. Two mountain ranges, the French Alps and the Pyrenees separate France from many countries, including Germany, Switzerland, Italy, and Spain. France's 22 regions offer a wide variety of natural features, including the Massif Central, a mountainous area with dormant volcanoes. At 634 miles (1,020 km) the Loire is France's longest river. The Seine River flows west through Paris, France's capital, to the Atlantic Ocean.

14

1

We'll start to draw the map of France by making a large square.

2

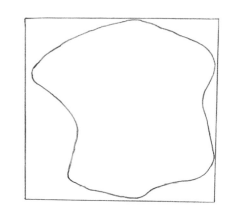

Look at the map on page 14 and draw a curved shape as an outline of the map.

3

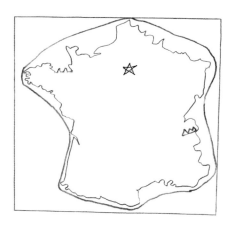

Next draw short, pointed lines inside the curved shape to show the boundaries of France. Add a star near the top center of the map to show where Paris is located. Add small mountain shapes at the right border to locate Mt. Blanc and the Alps.

4

Sketch a dotted line on the right to show the Rhone River then draw an upside-down *U* to show the location of Lascaux Cave.

5

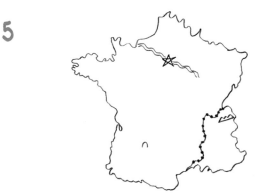

In the upper left corner, add four wavy lines set side by side to show the Seine River.

6

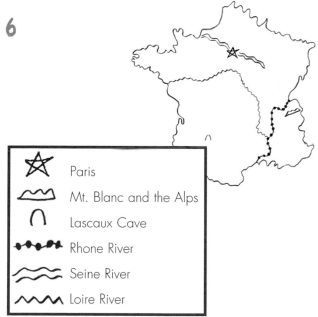

☆	Paris
⌒⌒	Mt. Blanc and the Alps
∩	Lascaux Cave
••••••	Rhone River
～～	Seine River
∧∧∧	Loire River

In the final step make a bumpy line across the map, as shown, to show the Loire River. Next draw a map key, or box that shows and labels some of the symbols of France.

Flag of France

The French call their flag *le tricolore*, or "the tricolor," which is a flag of three colors. The colors blue, white, and red are divided into vertical stripes of the same size. The red and blue stripes represent the capital, Paris. The white stripe is for the house of Bourbon, the French royal family that ruled from 1589 to 1792. The colors were first used together during the French Revolution in 1789. The colors of the flag also stand for liberty, or freedom.

The French Euro

Since January 1, 1999, the euro has been a form of currency, or money, that is used by several European countries. These countries are members of the European Union. All coins in the Union have the same front face to show how much the coin is worth. The other side of the coins have different designs. The design on the back is a Tree of Life. It is a symbol of growth and long life.

FLAG

1

Begin the French flag by drawing a rectangle.

3

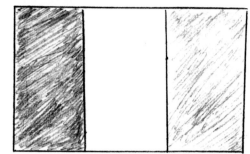

Shade using red for the first stripe, white in the middle, and blue for the last stripe.

2

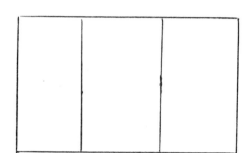

Draw two vertical lines.

EURO

1

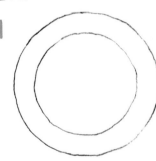

The design on the back side of the this euro coin is a tree that is the symbol of life and growth. Start with a circle inside another circle.

3

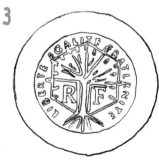

Draw a hexagon, or six-sided shape, around the tree. On the outside of the hexagon write the words "Liberté Egalité Fraternité." Add branches to the tree.

2

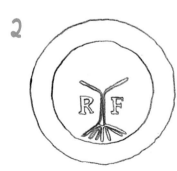

Begin the tree by drawing a large Y shape inside the inner circle. At the bottom of the Y, add seven lines for its roots. On either side of the trunk draw the letters R and F.

4

Finish drawing the euro coin by adding the stars between the outer and the inner circles. Connect the stars with diagonal lines.

Fleur-de-Lis

The origin of the fleur-de-lis, or "flower of the lily," is a mystery. Some believe the fleur-de-lis is an iris, which is a plant related to the lily. Both irises and lilies are shaped like a funnel and have large petals.

Some stories say that in the fifth century, Clovis, a very early king of France, received a golden lily from an angel when he became a Christian. Another legend says that Clovis picked a yellow iris from a riverbank on the way to battle and put it in his helmet as a symbol of his future victory.

Much later, during the twelfth century, either Louis VI or Louis VII became the first French king to use the fleur-de-lis on his shield. The fleur-de-lis may also have been called the flower of Louis. For centuries since then, the kings of France used the fleur-de-lis as their emblem, or crest, to mean perfection, light, and life.

1

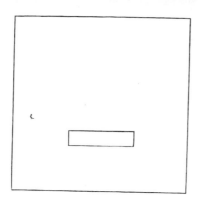

Start your drawing of a fleur-de-lis with a large square as a guide. Add a small horizontal rectangle inside.

2

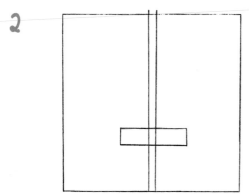

Next draw two parallel lines down the center of the square.

3

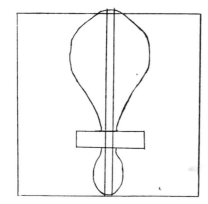

Next draw a large lightbulb shape above the small rectangle, and a smaller, upside-down lightbulb below.

4

Draw two curved shapes from the top of each side of the small rectangle. Draw smaller curved shapes below the rectangle.

5

Erase the square guideline to show the shape of the fleur-de-lis.

6

Finish your drawing with shading to show detail.

The Wild Horses of Camargue

Camargue is a marshland in the south of France by the Rhone River where herds of wild horses roam. The Camargue horse is among the oldest breeds of horses in the world. In fact, Camargue horses have existed in France since prehistoric times. They are fairly small horses and are very strong. They are able to endure bad weather and long periods without food. At birth their hair is either black or dark gray, but it turns either white or light gray after about five years.

Most Camargue horses are wild, though many are trained to take riders. French cowboys use the horses to round up the herds of bulls raised in Camargue. In 1928, the Camargue Regional Park was established to protect these horses and other wildlife.

1

To begin drawing the horse make a large oval.

2

Next draw a rectangle. Make sure that the bottom of the rectangle meets the bottom curve of the oval.

3

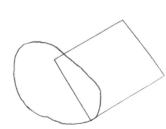

Add two long, thin rectangles at the bottom of the oval to make the legs. Next sketch the horse's head using the photo on page 20 as a guide.

4

Erase the outer rectangle, then add a small rectangle at the side of the head for an ear. Draw the shapes of the horse's front legs, then draw two long rectangles for the rear legs.

5

Erase the small rectangle guides for the front legs and sketch in the shapes of the rear legs. Draw the shapes of hooves at the bottom of each leg.

6

Erase the guides for the rear legs. Draw a pointed ear at the top of the head. Add small ovals for the eyes. Draw two nostrils, then an upturned line for the mouth.

7

Erase the small rectangle guide for the ear. To draw the horse's mane, sketch a wavy line from behind the head to the middle of the back.

8

Shade to show the horse's shiny coat. Darken the mane, the hooves, and circles around the eyes.

Grapes

Grapes grow on long, woody vines in fields called vineyards. France has millions of acres (ha) of vineyards. Grapes have been an important crop in France for more than 2,000 years. They have been eaten fresh, dried into raisins, and made into juice. They are also the ingredient of world-famous French wines.

France's climate is ideal for growing grapes. The summers tend to be warm and dry, which helps to ripen the fruit. The rich soil helps the roots and vines to grow strong. As they grow, the vines are tied to supports that keep them off the ground. The vines are pruned, or cut, each year to get rid of unwanted parts of the plant.

The regions in France that are best known for making fine wines are Bordeaux, Burgundy, Rhone, Champagne, Loire, and Alsace. The grapes in each region produce wines with their own individual flavors.

1

To draw the grapes and leaf we will start with a rectangle for a guide.

2

Draw the shape, as shown, which will be a guide to drawing a bunch of grapes. Add the first grape circle at the top of the shape.

3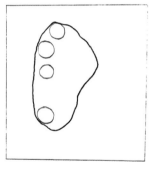

Add another three circles in the shape.

4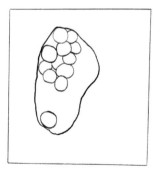

Continue to add more circles inside the shape. Grapes are the fruit of the plant. They carry the seeds.

5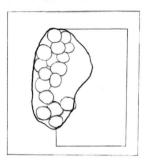

Start this step by drawing a rectangle behind your bunch of grapes to serve as a guide for a leaf. Add more circles as shown.

6

Erase the first rectangle. Inside the rectangle draw a wavy shape for the outline of the leaf. Add a few more circles for grapes.

7

Erase the rectangle.

8

To finish, shade the grapes so that they are dark and then add some light curved lines to show the veins of the leaf. Add more shading to the leaf, and you're done.

Lascaux Cave Paintings

Lascaux Cave is below the ground in Dordogne, a region in southwestern France. More than 15,000 years ago, Stone Age people painted the walls and ceilings of this cave with drawings of the animals that they hunted. Life-like bulls, deer, and horses were painted red, yellow, brown, and black. Some scientists believe that cave art was created as part of a magic ceremony to help hunters catch their prey. Many people believe that Lascaux has the most beautiful and famous cave paintings in the world. Four boys discovered the cave in 1940. The paintings had existed so long because the cave had been mostly sealed. Since the cave's discovery, scientists have been trying to find ways to preserve this priceless art.

1

To begin drawing a horse from a Lascaux cave painting, draw a large rectangle to serve as a guide.

2

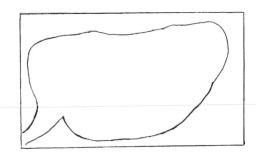

Next draw an oval shape with an opening at the left side of the rectangle.

3

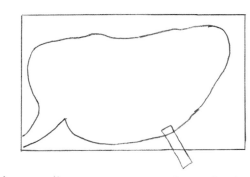

Add a small, narrow rectangle at the bottom right of the shape. It will become one of the horse's legs.

4

Next erase the outer rectangle. Add small, pointed shapes at the end of the back leg. Use the small rectangle to draw the front leg.

5

Erase the small rectangle and then add two more curved and pointed shapes for the other legs of the horse.

6

Erase a section of the oval at the right side to make space for the horse's neck. Draw small shapes on the ends of the legs to show the horse's hooves.

7

To make the horse's bushy mane, sketch many dark lines back and forth on the neck and what will be the head of the horse. Add five lines to indicate the the horse's nose. Add a long, curved line on the left for the horse's tail.

8

To finish, shade the body of the horse and darken the tail.

25

Pont du Gard

   Long ago, Roman chariots crossed the Pont du Gard. The Pont du Gard is a stone bridge that spans the Gard River between the towns of Uzés and Nîmes in southern France. The Romans, who had conquered France, built the bridge around the first century B.C. This 30-mile-long (48.3-km-long) bridge was part of an aqueduct, a system of channels and tunnels that provided water to Nîmes from a natural spring about 31 miles (49.9 km) north of the town.

   The Pont du Gard has three levels of arches and stands almost 160 feet (48.8 m) high, making it the highest Roman aqueduct in the world. It is 900 feet (274.3 m) long. This ancient wonder was built of stone, and is held together without the use of cement.

1

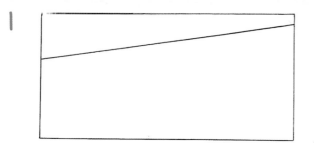

To draw the Pont du Gard, draw a rectangle. Draw a long diagonal line across the top third of the rectangle.

2

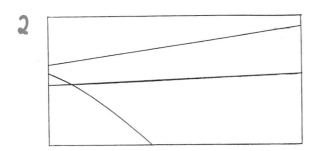

Draw a slightly angled line that almost divides the page in half. Add a slightly curved line at the left to serve as a guide for the riverbank.

3

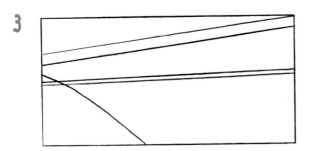

Add two lines next to the long horizontal lines drawn before.

4

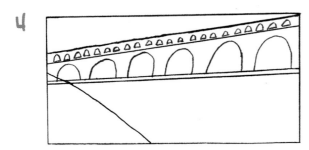

To create the top level of the bridge, draw tiny arches between the top two lines. Make larger arches by drawing large upside-down *U*'s above the two sets of straight lines.

5

Next draw the bottom level of the bridge with longer *arches*. Then draw wavy lines to suggest the outlines of plants growing on the riverbank.

6

At this point, erase the outside rectangle and the guide for the riverbank. To show that the bridge is made of cut stones, draw small rectangular shapes on the side of the upper and lower levels of the bridge.

7

Start to shade the bridge. Add shadows inside the arches to show depth. Make the shading of the riverbank darker than the bridge. Now you're finished.

Le Mont-Saint-Michel

Le Mont-Saint-Michel rises sharply to a height of 256 feet (78 m) from a bay along the English Channel. It is a rocky piece of land that becomes a small island at high tide. Le Mont-Saint-Michel got its name in the eighth century when a Christian bishop built a chapel there after seeing Saint Michael. When a monastery, built in 966, was partly burned in 1203, King Philip II paid for the construction of a monastery known as *La Merveille*, or the Wonder. Once the monastery was completed, huge walls were added in 1256 to stop attacking armies.

By the nineteenth century, Napoléon closed the monastery and turned it into a state prison. In 1874, the French established it as a historic monument.

1

Begin drawing Le Mont-Saint-Michel by making a large rectangle to use as a guide.

2

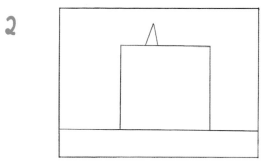

Draw a straight line across the lower part of the rectangle. Add a large square above the line. Add a small triangle on top of the square for the main steeple.

3

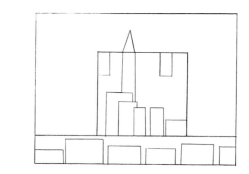

Add several rectangles of different sizes inside both the square and the rectangle to represent the buildings that make up the village of Le Mont-Saint-Michel.

4

Erase the top of the rectangle and part of the top of the square. Start to add straight lines and triangles to the tops of the buildings. These will be the roofs of the small buildings.

5

Erase inside guidelines. Draw some shapes with pointed tips around the church and other tall buildings. Draw curved lines behind the buildings to represent trees.

6

Add many rectangles for windows to all of the buildings. Erase the guides around the trees.

7

Draw a long oval shape in the tallest tower of the church to show the top window.

8

Shade the buildings. Finish by making the trees and rooftops dark.

29

Notre Dame Cathedral

Notre Dame Cathedral is considered the most famous Gothic cathedral in Europe. Gothic is a style of French architecture known for tall, pointed arches and high ceilings. Notre Dame was begun in 1163 and was mostly completed by 1250. The roof of the cathedral is 115 feet (35 m) high.

Sunlight shines through large stained, or colored, glass windows. Notre Dame has three round rose windows, which have designs made of stained glass and metal that date from the thirteenth century. Three doorways at the cathedral's west entrance are decorated with early Gothic-style carvings. Above them is a row of figures that represent kings from the Bible's Old Testament. Gargoyles look down from two square, 223-foot (68-m) towers that soar over the cathedral. These stone creatures are in the forms of frightening birds, dragons, and other monsters.

1

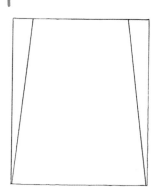

Begin by drawing the center of the cathedral with a rectangle. Draw two triangles at each side of the rectangle, with the wider ends at the top. The photo shows how the building becomes narrower at the top.

2

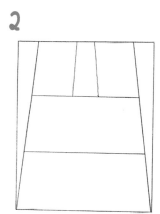

Draw two horizontal lines across the shape that was made by the triangles. From the top line, draw two slanted vertical lines to the top of the rectangle.

3

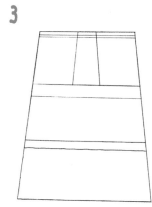

Erase the sides and the top corners of the rectangle. Add a line just below each of the the two horizontal lines you just drew. Add two more horizontal lines at the top of the rectangle.

4

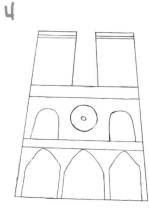

Erase the center lines at the top. In the middle section, draw two upside-down U shapes to represent windows. Between them draw two circles for the rose window. At the bottom, draw three pointed shapes.

5

Draw long, upside-down U-shaped windows in the towers at the top level of the cathedral. Add another line just below them for a ledge. Draw two lines on each side of the rose window. Add details in the windows on that level. Add doors to the bottom level.

6

Draw tiny lines for shading at the top of each tower. Draw small vertical lines on the ledges at each level. Add shading lines around the long windows at the top of the tower. Shade the tops of the doors on the bottom for depth. Draw lines in the rose window.

7

Continue shading to add depth and detail throughout the drawing. Notice the light and dark areas when shading. Make the windows and doors the darkest areas.

Half-Timbered Houses

Alsace, France, is a region of charming storybook villages. Alsace is close to Germany. During times of war, Alsace had been under German rule. It has many features seen in German villages, including half-timbered houses. Many half-timbered houses were built in the sixteenth century. The term comes from the practice of

using logs that were cut in half. Inside, the houses were usually made of oak. The outside walls of these houses were made of wattle and daub. Wattle is poles, branches, and reeds that have been bent and laced together to form different patterns. Daub, a soft, sticky, plasterlike substance, is used to fill in any holes in the timber. The houses were built on raised stone foundations and were topped with tile roofs. Today many are painted bright colors. Storks often nest in the chimneys, adding to the fairy-tale image.

1

Begin your drawing of a half-timbered house by drawing a large rectangle.

2

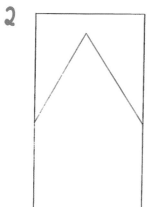

Next draw two lines that form a steep point above the middle of the page. They will eventually become the roof of the house.

3

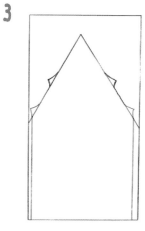

Draw four small pointed shapes, two on each side of the roof. From each of the bottom shapes, draw a long, straight line.

4

Erase the top and sides of the rectangle, to show the shape the house. Add three horizontal lines to make the different floors of the house. Add a curved line at the bottom right to outline the bush seen in the photo.

5

Draw a straight line just below each horizontal line.

6

Draw three small, narrow, side-by-side rectangles for windows at the third floor of the house. Add two long rectangles on the second floor. Draw wavy lines to outline the bush.

7

Erase the curved line guide. Draw a small square window at the top floor. Add two thin lines just below the windows on the second and third floors. Draw two windows, at the bottom floor of the house, that are partly hidden by the bush.

8

To finish the house, draw in details that show the wattle, or branches. Add shading around the windows. Shade the bush, and you're finished.

33

Joan of Arc

Joan of Arc was inspired to fight for her country even as a child. By 1428, England had conquered France during the Hundred Years War. That's when Joan, a 16-year-old farm girl, claimed that she heard saints telling her to save France. In 1429, dressed in armor, Joan of Arc led the French army to a victory at the town of Orléans. Shortly after, with Joan's help, the French crown prince took back his throne and was crowned King Charles VII. Enemies accused 19-year-old Joan of being a witch and had her burned to death. Her bravery and love for her country, however, gave the French army the will to drive the English out of France, ending the war by 1453. About 500 years later, the Catholic Church proclaimed her a saint. Many monuments were built to remember France's greatest heroine. The bronze statue to the left is in Paris. It shows Joan riding her horse, ready for battle.

1

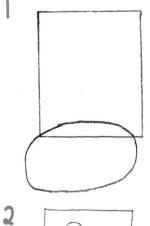

Begin the drawing of the statue of Joan of Arc by sketching a rectangle. Add an oval shape that overlaps the rectangle at the bottom.

2

In the rectangle draw the outline of the statue as seen in the photograph. Draw two long rectangles at the bottom of the oval. They will be the horse's legs.

3

Draw a slanted rectangle above the statue's left shoulder. This is a guide for drawing one of Joan's arms. Then draw the shapes of the horse's legs inside the long rectangles. Add more guides on the left and the right below the oval.

4

Sketch the shape of the statue's arm. For ears, draw two small rectangles on each side of what will be the horse's head. Add a curved line to show the outline of Joan of Arc's leg. Next draw the horse's other two legs.

5

Erase guidelines around the statue. Draw a long pole and add a rectangle with a small ball on top for the flag. Draw curved lines for Joan's hair and a slanted rectangle behind Joan. Draw the horse's ears, eyes, and mouth. Draw a wavy line around the horse's neck.

6

Sketch detail to give the flag its shape. Add detail inside the guides on the statue's back. Draw reins with curved lines around the horse's head and mouth. Add more detail to show the shape of Joan's armor. Draw lines for the horse's hooves.

7

Erase the flag rectangles. Draw curved lines to give additional detail to show Joan's armor. Draw an upside-down *U* for Joan's stirrups, at the bottom of her boot.

8

Using the picture as a guide, shade the drawing to give it depth and shadow. Make the horse's reins and hooves the darkest part of the drawing. Draw tiny lines to show Joan's hair.

Château de Chenonceau

Have you ever seen a castle float on air and water? The Château de Chenonceau seems to do just that. The château, or castle, is actually built over a river. It stretches across the Cher River in Chenonceaux, a tiny village in western France. Of all the many royal palaces in the Loire Valley, this one may be the most beautiful. A gallery, or long hall, was built over a bridge with five arches. Boats pass under the bridge and through the arches, traveling up and down the river. A two-story gallery in the castle was owned and designed by Catherine de Médicis, the wife of Henri II. It was completed in 1576. The gallery is connected to the front of the castle, which was built between 1513 and 1521. This square building has many turrets, or little towers, that stand over an old water mill. The castle also has one of the first straight staircases in France.

1

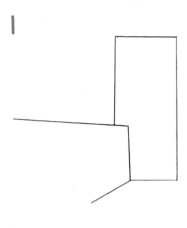

Begin your picture of the château by drawing a rectangle. In the lower left side of the rectangle, draw a wall with three lines.

2

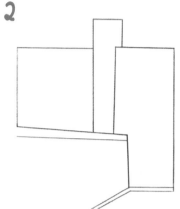

Draw two shapes next to the first, as shown. Add lines along the top and bottom of the wall, and at the bottom of the large rectangle.

3

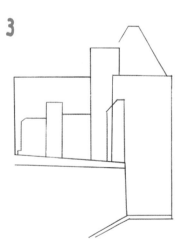

Above the large rectangle, draw a roof as shown. Draw four small shapes to show different sections of the château.

4

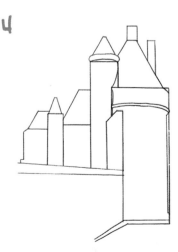

Inside the large rectangle draw curving lines to create a cylinder shape. Top each of the smaller rectangles with roofs as shown. Add small rectangles.

5

Add detail to the different sections of the château by drawing more lines and rectangles.

6

Draw tiny rectangles and long shapes for windows. Add more small, straight lines to the buildings to give them greater detail. Draw a small balcony in the center. Add tiny crosses atop the roofs.

7

Draw small, rectangular bricks on the wall and in several spots of the château buildings as shown. Draw an outline to show the shape of a large window at the bottom of the château.

8

Shade to darken all of the roofs of the buildings. Make the windows dark as well. Lightly shade the rest of the buildings. You've finished the château.

37

Napoléon Bonaparte

During the French Revolution, leaders in England and other European countries fought to keep the monarchy in France. The rulers were afraid that, if France became a republic, their subjects would want republics, too. In 1793, a French military leader named Napoléon Bonaparte took back a town that had been conquered by the British. After that success, he was made a general and he won many more battles against Italy and Austria by moving into the battlefield fast, fighting hard, and scattering the enemies' troops. When the revolution ended in 1799, Napoléon was France's new hero.

In 1799, France became a republic with Napoléon as its leader. In 1804, he made himself emperor and set out to conquer Europe. By 1811, Napoléon ruled all of western Europe, except England. His enemies fought back and Napoléon was forced to give up his power. Many monuments have been built to him, such as this bust of Napoléon in Corsica.

1
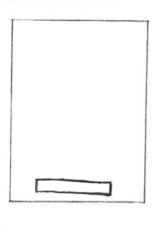
Start the bust of Napoléon by drawing a large rectangle as a guide. Add a small, horizontal rectangle near the bottom.

2

Add a large *U* shape above the rectangle.

3

Draw the outline of the head and shoulders of the bust above the *U* shape. Add straight lines to the rectangle to create a stand for the bust.

4
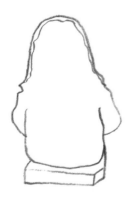
Inside the head of the bust, draw a wavy line to show some detail of Napoléon's hair.

5

Draw a wavy line from one shoulder to the other. This is the outline of a shirt. Draw a wavy shape to form the neck and chin. Draw two lines at the bottom for the belt.

6

Add a wavy *V* shape to give Napoléon's shirt more detail. Draw two lines from the left side to complete the belt.

7

Add more detail to the hair and face of the bust. Draw a curved line for a part in his hair. Draw two ovals for his eyes. Add eyebrows. Draw in his nose and lips.

8

Shade the bust by making dark, swirling shapes in the hair. Shade for more detail in his neck and face, and to give detail to the shirt.

The Arc de Triomphe

The *Arc de Triomphe* was truly meant to be an "arch of triumph." When Emperor Napoléon Bonaparte ordered its construction in 1806, he planned to have his army return in victory and march under the arch past cheering crowds. However, before the Arc de Triomphe was finished, Napoléon's rule ended.

The Arc de Triomphe, planned by architect Jean Chalgrin, was completed in 1836. At 164 feet (50 m) high and 148 feet (45.1 m) wide, it is the world's largest triumphal arch built to celebrate military triumph or victory. The Arc remembers World War I veterans with the Tomb of the Unknown Soldier and an eternal flame. The Arc is located at Place Charles de Gaulle in Paris.

1

Draw a large rectangle to serve as a guide for your drawing of the Arc.

2

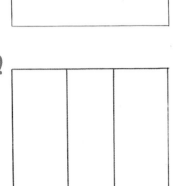

Draw two vertical lines to divide the rectangle into three equal sections.

3

Draw two lines across the middle of the rectangle. Erase the top halves of the two vertical lines. Make a large *U* shape above the middle lines.

4

Draw four horizontal lines across the arch, as shown. Add a small, ornamental circle just below the top of the arch.

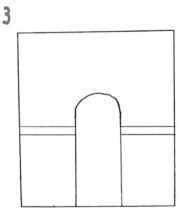

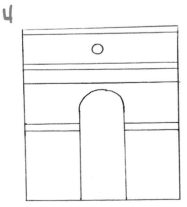

5

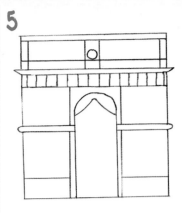

Draw straight lines for detail, 4 in the top section and 15 just above the arch. Add lines for detail and depth, as shown. Draw curved lines inside the arch.

6

Draw small lines above the top ledge and add small, decorative circles. Draw two rectangles on either side. Add wavy sculptures on each side.

7

Fill in the section below the top ledge, the two rectangles, and the sculptures with wavy lines for detail.

8

To finish the Arc de Triomphe, add shading to the drawing. Use the photo as a guide to make the light and dark areas.

The Eiffel Tower

The most famous symbol of Paris is the Eiffel Tower. Few things can compare to this modern wonder of the world. It is made from more than 18,038 strips of iron with huge gaps between them. The total weight of the Eiffel Tower is 10,100 tons (9,162.6 t), yet it is designed so that it places no more pressure on the ground than does a man seated on a chair.

Bridge engineer Alexandre-Gustave Eiffel created the oddly shaped tower, and it took about two years to build. This was just in time for the Paris Universal Exhibition, or world's fair, of 1889. The Eiffel Tower's three floors have restaurants, a museum, and glass elevators that rise on a curve to the top. You can also reach the top by climbing 1,655 steps. Until 1930, it was the world's tallest building. The height of the Eiffel Tower, including its television antenna, is 1,063 feet (324 m).

1

Start your drawing of the Eiffel Tower with a single vertical line to serve as a guideline.

2

Add two long, slightly curved vertical lines on either side of the straight line. Have the lines sweep out at the bottom.

3

Draw three straight horizontal lines through the structure, one near the top and two in the lower section, as shown.

4

Add another five horizontal lines through the structure. These lines are the beginnings of the levels of the ironwork on the Eiffel Tower.

5

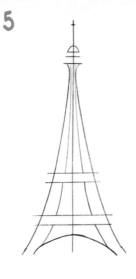

Using the second line, draw a half circle on the antenna at the top of the tower. Draw another set of long, sweeping lines from the top to the bottom of the structure. Draw a curved line half circle at the bottom of the structure. This will form the bottom of the Eiffel Tower.

6

Erase the bottom of the original vertical line. Add a small, rectangular shape near the top of the tower. Add vertical and horizontal lines between the lines you drew earlier. Draw lines above the bottom arch. Add a row of X's and lines for design details throughout the tower.

7

Complete the Eiffel Tower by adding more X's in each of the boxes that you created to show all the detail. Shade the arch for depth. Then lightly shade the interior. Add five small lines at the top to show the light on the antenna.

Timeline

50 B.C.	The Romans, led by Julius Caesar, conquer France (then called Gaul).
486	The Franks, people from Germany, conquer the Romans, then name and occupy France.
1337–1453	France and England fight the Hundred Years War.
1429	Joan of Arc leads the French army against the English.
1643–1715	King Louis XIV, the Sun King, rules France, Europe's most powerful country.
1789–1799	The French Revolution begins.
1804	Napoléon is crowned emperor of France.
1815	Napoléon is defeated at the Battle of Waterloo.
1914–1918	Germany invades France during World War I. France, the United States, England, and Russia win the war, but many people die and France is in ruins.
1944	On June 6, D-Day, a major battle of World War II, is fought on the beaches of Normandy, France. Paris is freed from German control in August.
1958	Charles de Gaulle becomes president.
1999	The euro, the single European currency, is launched.

France Fact List

Official name	French Republic
Area	212,918 square miles (551,455 sq km)
Continent	Europe
Population (2000)	About 60.4 million
Capital	Paris
Most-Populated City	Paris, population 2,125,246
Industries	Steel, machinery, chemicals, automobiles, and aircraft
Agriculture	Wine grapes, wheat, cereals, dairy products, fish
National anthem	"La Marseillaise"
Official language	French
Common Phrase	*Bonjour,* "good day"
Currency	Euro
National holiday	Bastille Day, July 14
Most popular sport	Soccer
Popular dish	Bouillabaisse, a fish stew
Longest river	Loire River, 634 miles (1,020.3 km)
Major lake	Lake Geneva, 224 square miles (580.2 sq km)
Highest peak	Mont Blanc, 15,771 feet (4,807 m)
Major religions	Roman Catholicism, Protestantism, Islam, Judaism
Boundaries	Italy, Switzerland, Spain, Germany, Luxembourg, Belgium, the Mediterranean Sea, the Bay of Biscay, the Strait of Dover, the North Sea, the Atlantic Ocean, and English Channel.

GLOSSARY

achievements (uh-CHEEV-ments) Great things that are done by hard work.

aqueduct (A-kweh-dukt) A channel or pipe used to carry water long distances.

architecture (AR-kih-tek-cher) Designing and making buildings.

armor (AR-mer) A type of uniform used in battle to help protect the body.

bishop (BISH-ep) A clergyman ranking above a priest.

canvases (KAN-ves-ez) Cloth surfaces that are used for paintings.

cathedral (kuh-THEE-druhl) A Large church that is run by a bishop.

ceremony (SER-ih-moh-nee) A special series of actions done on certain occasions.

château (sha-TOH) A large country house or a castle in France.

culture (KUL-chur) The beliefs, practices, art, and religions of a group of people.

dangerous (DAYN-jer-us) Able to cause harm.

dormant (DOR-muhnt) Resting, not active.

emblem (EM-bluhm) A picture with a motto.

emperors (EM-per-erz) The rulers of empires, or several countries.

empire (EM-pyr) A large area under one ruler.

foundation (fown-DAY-shun) The part on which other parts are built.

French Revolution (FRENCH reh-vuh-LOO-shun) A time of very important change and fighting that began in France in 1789.

gargoyle (GAR-goylz) Carved, animal-like figures with scary faces.

Gothic (GAH-thik) A style of making buildings, popular from the twelfth to the early sixteenth century.

heroine (HER-uh-wun) A woman or girl who is brave, does good things, and has a noble character.

high tide (HY TYD) The time when ocean water is highest on the shore.

landmarks (LAND-marks) Important buildings, structures, or places.

landscapes (LAND-skayps) Views of scenery on land.

literature (LIH-tuh-ruh-chur) Writings such as novels, plays, or poetry.

marshland (MARSH-land) Soft, wet land.

masterpieces (MAS-tur-pees-es) Anything done or made with wonderful skills.

migrate (MY-grayt) When large groups move from one place to another.

monastery (MAH-nah-ster-ee) A house where people who have taken religious vows live and work.

parliament (PAR-lih-mint) The lawmakers of a country.

prehistoric (pree-his-TOR-ik) The time before written history.

prime minister (PRYM MIH-nih-ster) The leader of a government.

republic (ree-PUB-lik) A form of government in which authority belongs to the people.

resources (REE-sors-ez) A supply or source of energy or useful materials.

revolution (reh-vuh-LOO-shun) A complete change in government.

royalty (ROY-ul-tee) Relating to a king, queen and their family.

scorned (SKORND) To have looked down upon.

spans (SPANZ) Covers the length of something, such as a bridge.

Stone Age (STOHN AYJ) A time when very early humans used tools and weapons.

symbols (SIM-bulz) Objects or designs that stand for something else.

vertical (VUR-tih-kul) In an up-and-down direction.

vineyards (VIN-yurdz) Areas in which grapes are grown.

World War I (WURLD WOR WON) The war fought between the Allied Powers and the Central Powers from 1914 to 1918.

World War II (WURLD WOR TO) A war fought between the United States, Great Britain, France, and Russia, and Germany, Japan, and Italy from 1939 to 1945.

INDEX

WEB SITES

Due to the changing nature of Internet links, PowerKids Press has developed an online list of Web sites related to the subject of this book. This site is updated regularly. Please use this link to access the list:
www.powerkidslinks.com/kgdc/france/